PowerKids Readers:
My World™

My Breakfast
A Book About a Great Morning Meal
Heather Feldman

The Rosen Publishing Group's
PowerKids Press™
New York

1

For Karen, Paul, and Lynn—my second family

Published in 2000 by The Rosen Publishing Group, Inc.
29 East 21st Street, New York, NY 10010

First Edition

Book design: Danielle Primiceri

Photo Illustrations by John Bentham

Feldman, Heather L.
    My breakfast : a book about a great morning meal/ by Heather Feldman.
      p. cm. — (My world)
      Includes index.
      Summary: A boy describes how he eats his favorite breakfast, cereal with milk and juice and sometimes toast with jam.
      ISBN 0-8239-5527-3
      1. Breakfasts—Juvenile literature. 2. Cereals, Prepared—Juvenile literature. [1. Cereals, Prepared. 2. Breakfasts. 3. Food habits.] I. Title. II. Series: Feldman, Heather L.
My world.
TX733.F45   1998
641.5'2—dc21
                            98-31956
                                CIP
                                AC

Manufactured in the United States

Contents

I love cereal for breakfast.
I pour milk on my favorite
cereal in my favorite bowl.

I always eat my favorite cereal with my favorite spoon.

I always need a glass of my favorite juice to go with my favorite cereal.

Sometimes I have toast with my favorite cereal and my favorite juice.

I spread my favorite jam on my toast. My favorite jam is blueberry.

A good breakfast every morning helps me start my day!

I love cereal for breakfast!

My favorite cereal is all gone now.

19

I am ready to go to
school.

Words to Know

 BOWL

 BREAKFAST

 GLASS

 JAM

 JUICE

 MILK

 SPOON

 TOAST

22

Here are more books to read about breakfast:
The Berenstain Bears Cook-It: Breakfast for Mama
by Stan and Jan Berenstain
Random House, Inc.

To learn more about a good breakfast, check out these Web sites:
http://www.wraltv.com/features/healthteam/1997/0807-kidseat-part2/

Index

Word Count: 95

Note to Librarians, Teachers, and Parents

PowerKids Readers are specially designed to get emergent and beginning readers excited about learning to read. Simple stories and concepts are paired with photographs of real kids in real-life situations. Spirited characters and story lines that kids can relate to help readers respond to written language by linking meaning with their own everyday experiences. Sentences are short and simple, employing a basic vocabulary of sight words, as well as new words that describe familiar things and places. Large type, clean design, and photographs corresponding directly to the text all help children to decipher meaning. Features such as a picture glossary and an index help children get the most out of PowerKids Readers. Lists of related books and Web sites encourage kids to explore other sources and to continue the process of learning. With their engaging stories and vivid photo-illustrations, PowerKids Readers inspire children with the interest and confidence to return to these books again and again. It is this rich and rewarding experience of success with language that gives children the opportunity to develop a love of reading and learning that they will carry with them throughout their lives.